OLD TOWN CLOWN

THIRD EDITION

BY: TOD PERRY

POET @ MM22

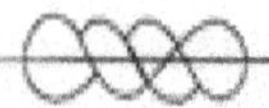

Wish I were more
Peter Lorre-ish, tho
a pickled onion or
Danny DeVito will do.
Clearly all three are
forever to remember,
while this haphazard rhyme
might not over time
grow on you, tall
like hair with a cow lick,
old puns and opinions
from the likely last
and first Poet Laureate
at Mile Marker 22,
his worn pony trick
to hop on two feet,
while hoping still later
(more razzle dazzle)
to stick on your wall
spaghetti and garlic.

TABLE OF CONTENTS

SECTION ONE: EARLY

TODDY

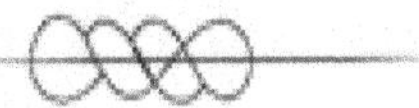

TODDY--A name given by my mother, born Frances Ann O'Sullivan,

and the only name I knew. My great grandfather from Cork was Timothy O'Sullivan. Possibly he was the same Timothy O'Sullivan who was the one time mayor of Cork, also known as Toddy, whose grandson Timothy O'Sullivan, again also informally, a Toddy.

This Toddy was a long time manager and famous host to generals and presidents at the prestigious Gresham hotel on O'Connell Street in Dublin. Will never know, but I left a note at the hotel, hoping someday it will be picked up and read by an O'Sullivan with some answers.

TODDY

--Bill Dickey

T is for the trouble that you gave me
O is for obscenity and sin
D is for delirium and tremens
D is for disaster marching in
Y is for the yogurt in the garden
put them all together they spell chaos

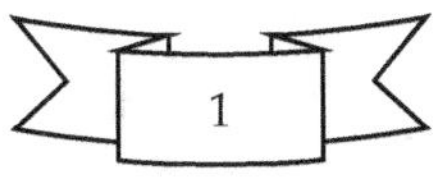

a word that means the world to me.

+

(From the men's room, Kenny's Bar, Iowa City, 1961-1963,Probable
author-Quentin Black)

Whiz bang, Poon tang,
wobbly ha, frog fart
push cart, Shangri la.

ELMORRO

---Puerto Rico

On calmer days
you can see from the tower
looking down fortress walls
sharks on patrol in the clear
green Atlantic waters.

The sea is calm today,
unusually calm,
long waves sweep ashore
rise up through boulders in spouts,
then rush back to sea
in walls rolling backward.

All day the swells
beat down, and twist
through porous stones,
on some pulse becoming
small lakes and pools
then plunge back down again,

Above, the fortress endures,
thick, impervious to centuries

of time and tide. Inside its walls
we worm in its intricate tunnels
through chambers, barracks, chapels
by delicate curving arches
cantilevered ceilings above
circular stairwells.

The dungeon is below
a grey cavity cut into stone
that speaks little of the past,
one small portal, a splash of light
through the bars of a webbed shaft.

A telescope set in stone
fixed on the sea it stares
at one circle of the sea.
No shore, no sky or waves.
The walls are bare, all washed
of the dragons and swift frigates
painted once in blood. All dreams
sandblasted away from the men
whose sails swelled each day with hope
from the sea until their eyes went blind,
searching the one circle of a deep sea
as life bled out into the green surface
of clear water where sharks still swim.

FOR NICHOLAS, BORN IN SEPTEMBER

Originally published in The New Yorker

You bring the only changes to this season.
Once more, Gomorrah has enjoyed its harvest;
old cards, discarded dominoes and chips
lie scattered on the patio; the beach
is quiet, half of its shells brought home to fade
like negatives. For miles the day is empty,
given to gulls that slide along the wind
and stab the shore. And I recall the way
so many autumns came. Bulbs on a cord
tottering upside down like icicles
above the wooden bandstand, a scarf of sand,
curling, begins to bury the cement.

We used to play there, in and out like moths
among the dancers, but more often owls,
perching along the edge of night, we'd screech
and try to disapprove of what we saw.
Our parents told us that before the war
the town was better, and certainly with time,
things would improve; their dignity was silence,
and summers lean and lifeless as the winter
afternoons. Now you have proved the future
falls in slow progressions of the present.

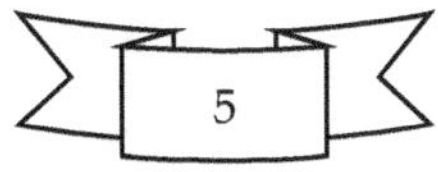

Tod Perry

The night the season ended, on Labor Day,
campfires roasted strings of unsold oysters
they'd given to us free. We'd watch sparks lift
across the fire, then finally disappear.
By morning the dancers were no longer there.

For two weeks after Labor Day, we'd spot
great herds of porpoises leap up the coast
in rain and ride out like September clouds.
Always, before, it was the saddest month,
the beach and water one monotonous sea
of careless stirrings and transparencies,
the cool breezes turning the white dunes gray.

Today, I saw a red oak tree—the one
they planted when the war was won—its leaves,
stubborn as winter, clawing in the wind
as if to tear it down. The tree in time
collapsed among the barren upright elms,
but watching it drop here reminded me
how soon the days adjusted to the fall
and settled in to wait like seeds till June,
when porpoises return, salting the tides.

My first born, the 18th of September
of my only season, you have risen
like a sapling among these barren trees.
Each day I watch you spread the deepest roots
in our common soil; I touch you with my hand,

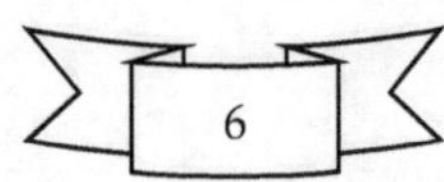

veined and strong as a leaf. This time I feel
a wind I never knew blow through my bones.

Tod Perry

FOURTH OF JULY

And my first is nearly four.
Explosions in the sky to celebrate
our destiny of peace from strength.
He sleeps below on pillows,
assurances against a darkness
hardly noticed under the parachutes
of sparks and the roar of hot rods
that gun through the streets and flip
loud cherry bombs from lawn to lawn.

Awake, alone, I keep my vigil
hoping the hammering soon ends,
knowing this flaming canopy
has made the neighbors feel secure
safe as my swaddled son, his cheek
still red from the scratch of my beard.

Red flashes late into the night,
the blasts all seem so deadly real,
and I, the discovered enemy within,
race inside the tunnels of my mind
where thousands more escape the lethal sky.

At last a dimness spreads from house to house

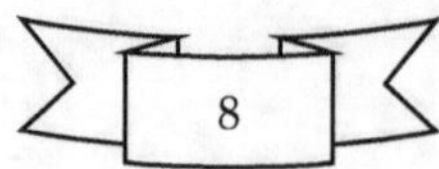

the neighborhood can safely rest,
no more parades no marching songs
no shadowed hint of a single doubt,
or one unthinkable truth to wrestle.

Not a splinter blows out from my dreams
where families crawl in villages of fire,
and bombardiers above can celebrate
the perfect patterns from a distance high
the web of fire floating down below.

In their dreams only heroes fly
their sparkling angels sit beside.
Full faith in what they're told, no fears
disturb their own now sleeping here
safe as candles that flicker on a cake,
guarded within a faith and affirmation
that shields each heart turned into sheets.

Tod Perry

IN THE EYE OF SPRING

A wild thing, this bird
that stares into my eyes.
I think almost it thinks,
but no, she's simply watching out,
and so, when I return her look, my eyes,
blue isles in white and pink
that tell the world of Ireland's snakes,
in a language mine, and yet to me unknown,
she bounces off a bit less near,
to keep an eye, a watchful stare.

So too my crafty heart
all peeks and nods
whistles in your direction,
to sing full voice far off
of wildness tamed by love.

NICHOLAS IN THE SUNROOM

Originally published in Prairie Schooner

Paisley and shimmering, the sunlight flows,
bending with his meanders across the room,
over the shadows of tentative green plants.
He poises hand and heel upon his ground,
a jackknife: snaps; rebalances his arms,
then tumbles down, a vine without a stake.
His bones are limber, and all predicaments.
Fancy: sunflower, turtle, frog or snake.
I would support his growth and watch it bloom,
this stake of mine, into the heart of life.

The sun, reptilian, parasitic, flows
to where he twists and pivots round himself—
his leafy hands and curving arms spread out
to catch the liquid currents of the air.
So much amuses and escapes his hands.
He fingers what is angular and sharp
and cannot know how brittle all things grow
within his arc of light. He cannot stare
at sunlight, nor evade it, but I have jammed
this stake of mine into the heart of life

THE BUTTERFLY

--Frances Ponge (translation by Tod Perry)

When the sugar, made in the stems, surges to the bottoms
of the flowers, as in badly rinsed cups, a great agitation
takes place on the ground--all at once the butterflies rise to the air.

The heads of the caterpillar turn to blind and eyeless casts; their
skins turn limp and shrivelled
from the explosive blaze of their wings
that litter and break out as twin flames.

From now on the fanciful butterfly only stops, as if
by accident, to pose on whatever hazards come its way.

A flying match, its flame is not catching. Besides,
it comes too late, and now can only endorse that the flowers are in
bloom. No matter: bobbing above them
like a lamptorch, it checks each one's store of oil,
and drops on the flower's crown its useless, tattered
coat, and so avenges its long, formless humiliation
as the caterpillar at the feet of the stems.
Miniature sailboat of the air, ill treated by
the currents of the wind, vagabond petal, it
has the run of the garden.

THE DEPARTURE

to K.P.

Originally published in EPOCH Magazine

Now you are gone and much of you is left
In this weather wind and tree hang
In the air, the high crooked branches lean
Headlong into space and ride the clouds.

The storm came on, the heavy metal weather
And gray rain ran like shadows thick in the trees;
Unbuckled as a leaf, whirling in a fear,
Your image severed in multiple pools;
Now only ripples tell us where we are.

Tod Perry

THE MUTE CRIPPLE
NOBODY KNOWS IS INSANE

Originally published in Prairie Schooner

Propped up in bed, I rest in 'the vegetable garden,'
among the basket cases, and other cases with useless limbs;
my eyes stare out the window. The Sunday visitors, arriv-
ing punctually early, crowd through the archway in a single
body, agile as a roach.

They cannot see me watching, but think— "perhaps" --
and wave.

The room they enter has the air of fabled Egyptian
tombs: the slightest movement toward my interior corner,
for instance, disrupts the columnar dust that has lain
in images all week in its shaft of sunlight, In that
way I know they have entered.

The statues I spent all week making out of the dust
with my eyes are washed away. Smiling, they bring a paint-
ing to hang. One hammers the wall, and..."oops". "What
happened?" He hit his thumb. "Did it hurt?", they ask.
It's bleeding some. And throbbing too? I say cut it off,
but don't say a word one way or the other.

I can watch the picture this week. Flowers in a Vase,
How heavy they look, drooping their petals gracelessly
from the tips of their stems. Flowers! This week swollen
thumbs, plant pickers, visiting relatives, and smiling

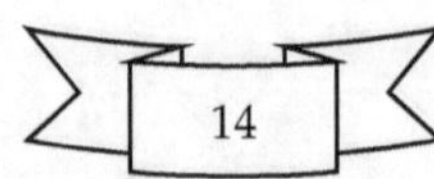

office seekers must be put in perspective. I will entomb them in the dust. Let them enter upon themselves when they visit.

THE OYSTER

--Francis Ponge (translated by Tod Perry)

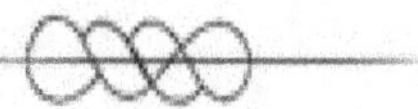

The size of a handy pebble, the oyster is coarser looking, and, though of less clear cut coloring, brilliantly chalkish. It is a stubborn, closed world. Still, it can be opened: you have to put it in the fold of a rag, start in on it with a rugged and slightly crooked blade, and keep at it for several tries. The prying fingers get sliced, and fingernails snap off: It is a tough kind of work. The pounding you have to give it stamps its casing with white rings, a sort of halo.

Once there on the inside you find a whole world to drink and to eat: a firmament (literally speaking) of mother of pearl, the sky above bent over the sky below, forming no more than a small pond, a viscous khaki bag that ebbs and rises in sights, in smells, fringed with a blackish lace along the edges.

On rare occasions, within the nacreous throat, this formula becomes a pearl, suddenly.

THE SOLID RAINFALL, BREAKING

Originally published in Contact

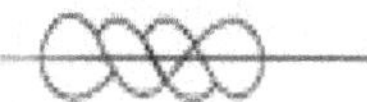

There must be a woman behind all this rain.
Nothing here is certain, nor what it seems.
The solid rainfall, breaking, shifts in patterns
on the avenues, bunches, spreads and roams
like trapezoids of sunlight over water.
Bright geometric figures of the rain,
once gone, they return in altered forms
to conjure up the shapes that fell before
and cannot be remembered. Flatter, wider,
the circles turn to squares and back again.
Proportion shifts as in a memory
or dream turned intricately flawed. Meaning
grows old, inverted and effeminate,
depending on the way the rainfall leans.

The raindrops land now in the outline of a smile,
but everything is suspect, even shapes
I can identify by name and place.
A woman I knew once, with her quiet face
on Japanese prints, where jewels and spiny birds
arrange on trees. She is that strange and silken.
So many patterns of her face arise,
precise before they prove inaccurate, dissolve,
and complicate the graceful rain.

Tod Perry

Her gestures haunt my head, like drifting moods
and scatter in the geometric shapes
where nothing's lost, exact or long. One learns,
finding each familiar, before they fly,
why in Oriental art the dark birds
rest in crooked patterns on the trees.

WHAT THE BEACH TOLD

Probably late October, November
when the North Atlantic pokes
its icy fingers inside of coats
one moment crispy sand and sunlight,
then spotty mixes of cloud,
cold chills, part gray, part rain.

The beach now harder on its foamy edges,
a cold cement, no longer gives beneath
the heels of children who chase in mobs
through cones of twisting sand in spirals
to whip their faces raw with salty grains--
sand for the eyes from a season turning harder.

A season to weather them no matter their speed
up the dunes, what secret paths in the weeds.
Loose as wind in wind, free of the eyes
on land, bound only by the waves rolling
to shore from distant waters to bear them gifts,
back and forth all day with the pipers to sift
what treasures ride on tides of endless ocean
all free, all theirs, and all for the keeping.

To fight off cold they invented clever tools,
two shells doubled in one hand to dig wider holes,

walls of thick sand still wet but reinforced
with sticks bound tight by weeds, strong forts
as shields against the ocean gusts that swirl
while they snuggle in warm puddles of sun below,
the blasts above made cozy as mild breezes.

Here was freedom, a world of their own to taste,
to drift all day on a beach, the gift of free food.
You could pluck it from the waves. It floated in:
K-rations, C-rations, meals in sea worthy coats
of wax: cheeses, crackers, chocolates, and cigarettes.
Incoming forbidden dreams and always more.

Always on top of the waves soon after the nights
when balls of orange flame burst on the horizon
where U-boats prowled the dark for liberty ships
lumbering in a black Atlantic, on to England
and terrors beyond in a mysterious Europe.

The flames were neon signals, jackpots awash
a bounty to float up soon onto the beaches
where scavengers and crabs danced upon a wreckage
of weapons dressed up in black cakes of tar,
life jackets soaked full heavy, dripping sea weed.
Sopping shapes on the sand, bloated, tangled
with things that cling to other things dead,
on pots and pans, the shattered beams of boats,
all treasure blackened by the burning waves,
and still danger and death seemed always far

yet some way connected by tide to this world
now growing fast into a winter moving closer.

One day when the sand and the wind seemed one
and peppered the eyes with sprays of buckshot,
they stumbled on it first, before they saw it,
no form, no up or down, all covered in slime
with the shape of a claw but maybe a tail.

Too tough and sticky to strip it off bare handed
or dig down deep with two shells cupped together,
they needed sticks, a smoother, sharper kind,
the strong ones used to spear a hardshell crab
to punch holes down clean through into the center,
to find the core of this fishy, smelling lump
pushed by winter wind and tides to an edge
of a barrier spit just off Long Island at war.

At first one jab but nothing opened, again,
poke after poke, deeper down and harder
through thick skins of tar to get into the heart,
so many holes so slick and all glittering
black eyes winking the flashes of sunlight,
hot-- until suddenly the blob became
a boy, a man, an enemy submariner
adorned in the bright jewelry of the oceans,
black eyes brilliant where no eyes were
that raced them up the dunes with their dazzling news
back home for those who knew, and were waiting.

SECTION TWO: LOST AND FOUND

US VS THEM

-- a bee bop boogie

Be a Bee and bop a Bop.
Be a Bop and bop a Bee.

Tod Perry

A FRIEND SPEAKS
OF UNREQUITED LOVE

Originally published in Key West I Love You

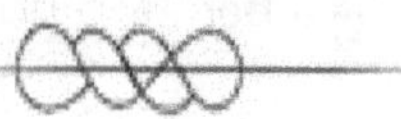

Unrequited love is to life
the tender inside of an oyster,
a room not lived in fully
until empty of all but pain
that grows heavy on the heart,
a pearl into a manhole cover,
an injury cradled by time,
no matter the weight,
a carapace that opens
in mist and shadows
of sorrows that cling
long behind, then move
slowly as you move
one room to the next

HE FOUND FREEDOM, THEN ESCAPED

-Rollin, d., 1989

Defiant as horns,
the commands from the big guy
goose step down the paths
of yesterday's paradise,
to echos of our wild games
of Ring-O, Ring-O Leave-E-O.

The sky is a puzzle now;
pieces of it fall. Leaves,
down early in the mountain silence,
and stars are scattered in the night,
in a jigsaw seen through barren limbs
where a spider on a secret path shuttles
across a missing moon on nets of silk,
spun from the breath of patience
tumbling into its own astrology,
filling absence with dark direction,
and deadly lines that fish for the heart.

Time dropping on a thread,
fisherman, stalker,
cat in a web,
gleam in the eye,

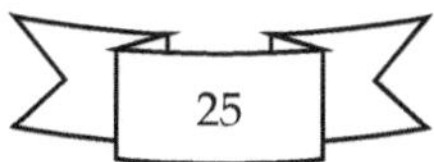

claw sharp as light,
the hidden spider came to fiddle
toyed with the brother who was little,
struck the big guy, the one in the middle.

A static in the air, you can feel him near,
that voice, his body charging headlong,
anyway at once, sideways, backwards,
a spinning basketball in motion,
energy first and then direction,
jumping Jack Flash and storms of will
then lightening striking from the shadows.

Time Out!
Who's that, running around?

Who blew that whistle?
That out-of-time
before his feet could hit the ground?

Whether hungry for life or love,
he found his freedom, and then escaped.
Embracing all but always seeking more
for fear of none, he rushed to take
and rushed to give it all he had,
and left the wake of what he is
behind in the wake of what it is.

At ease or rowdy, sober or demanding

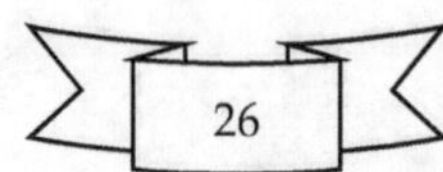

Old Town Clown

winking, through tears and laughter,
his hours were flares towering on our paths,
a flash so bright and sure to strike
we anticipate his follow through---
that charmer leaping from the shadows
he left with us and blazing brighter still,
that brassy cadence getting down and going on,
to dance again to the brontosaurus stomp,
to weave some more through the Star Wars bars
before the good times go to worm, to roar
while the joint is rocking with his echoes still.

Tod Perry

ONE INSTANT WITH THE WIND

The field I wander wags
like the tails of dogs
racing in the wind.
I feel myself swaying,
a tassel late on the stalk
brittle from winter,
free to speed wherever.

The season's come when wind
flies like an arrow out of town,
but ice still crackles under foot.

A wonder that the March wind
finds me drifting with the gusts
on the thawing edge of town
where bare trees butt the winds,
and Spring so long away.

Across the river, the banks
are packed with autumn leaves,
thick with gangs of boys,
their box kites sent up to climb
on cord high into the sky,
in one instant becoming
small doorways to an open sky,

diving in circles again and again
with the wind waving back to the boys
bobbing, pointing and waving below.

Tod Perry

SCRANTON

Trees tops cover the depressions of the hills,
a shawl of green for worn and wounded shoulders,
that shield the scars of Scranton's abandoned pits
rooted underneath the skyline of the valley
and keep secrets locked inside like prison walls.

Tall trees to hide what was taken over years,
the blasted hills and holes disguised by leaves,
so what is lost is lost to memory too,
A show of green that cannot patch such absence,
such wounds so deep in men and mountains both.
Nor can the flowers blooming on tops of slag piles,
bright blossoms in the snowy depth of winter
pyramids smoking in clusters along the tracks

Fumes and blooms in ice, Dickson on Scot Road,
decrepit scaffolds, beltways, rusted derelicts
they still hoist coals hot from the smoking mines,
leftovers of a lawless time when combines blasted
volcanic powders to break into the veins of ore.

At home in the valley, born to vapors and grit,
children of the locked out generations are rooted,
nowhere to go and ready first for any war,
each town the same today as long ago

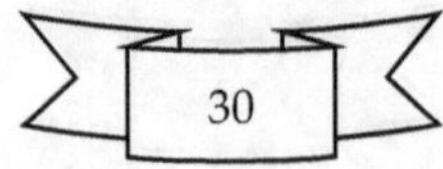

when Polish taverns sang to celebrate
the many goodbyes of sailors and their girls,
and plenty dressed in matching sailor suits
who danced to polkas with a whirling fire
seen here and nowhere else unless in Warsaw.

Patched for another year, the breakers stand,
iron donkeys with long beards of hanging soot
ready to crush the anthracite riding the belts
in loads cranked up still hot from Dickson's Pits.

Working in the "dog holes" --shut mines, (rogue active)—
small gangs of hasty hires-- those dogs with jobs--
scrape wages out of stone, for the dwindling profits
of wildcat owners who only measure risk
as coins to gain, and costs to cut or save.

The old dogs work in darkness, but now for less
for longer hours than laws allow, or not at all,
the rules of safety dead in webs and loopholes,
in the feeble concessions wrestled from a golden age
when combines that struck it rich were quick to scalp
the fast coal from the top, and left the roots for others,
underground, to gnaw, as burning, wriggling fuses
of lingering fire, to smoulder cave to cave.

Silent in the Susquehanna valley, in shafts
the jungle vines of abandoned fires climb
to flare at times as puffs of purple smoke

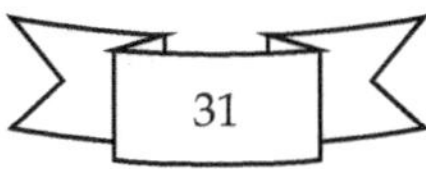

in squares of towns, to bloom in Carbondale,
to hollow out the porous bedrock of the valley,
to swallow homes-- they slant at first, then drop
first one, then two into the earth below.

In sister city, Wilkes-Barre in '59,
the Susquehanna overran its banks,
rapids raging into brittle veins of coke,
old dogs flushed down sinkholes, mine by mine,
dogs washed through caves, until finally plugged
by freight cars stuffed with slag, forever sealed.

Frontier cities from a century raised on hope,
these junk heap towns, torn hills, the tilted houses
are candles melted on dreams of easy wealth,
deserted as they aged with pride kept deep.
It burns inside, uncharted, out of sight,
a secret fire hidden in this slicker age
of harsher laws and even meaner terms.

With a grip still strong, hardened by icy winters
the valley grasps at any promise of renewal,
finds hope in roots and broken stones, in blooms
that stand against the cold on top of ashes,
those hands that chopped out livings from the pits,
those fists could wrench that wealth that wanders still.

SECTION THREE: RESTART

THE RULE OF THE DOG

... V. Putin

At a certain point
when a dog has a bone
it's his to howl
a rule to the point
making clear as a growl
which dog owns the bone.

CONSIDER THE JELLY FISH

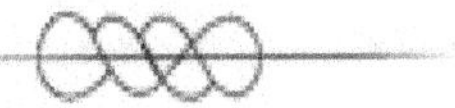

Squeeze too hard,
a jellyfish rolls out your knuckles,
squirts through your fingers.
Would you do that?
Never mind.
the choice is there, the what
do with fragile things before they fall apart.

They must have taught me something,
those armies that washed in glowing
through the ocean's doors spread over the shore
in a mix of spots of tar and tufts of foam
and sometimes carried to the dunes
with broken shells on waves.

Yanked ashore by change of current,
wobbly underfoot, these slimy carpets
are safe from the beaks of terns
but not the angry rays of a sun
that turns them into crispy skins.

A coat of sand can keep them cool,
you can touch them then,
trace their inner architecture,
jellied patterns of nerve and vein,

dead end vestige of tail, the seeds
of copper-headed monkey fish,
red dots, orange dashes of anything
there ever was or yet might be.

Oozing, sticky, shapeless,
fresh as incoming tide to the nose,
this immortal ball of code
can be read.
Hold it both hands, keep
eyes steady, as it wobbles,
breathe in, deep.

CUDJOE TWILIGHT, A WATERCOLOR

Wings hang sturdy
hands onto winds
they sway, swoop,
jittery kites,
disappear.

Frigate, Osprey, Pelican,
ah, the gulls, keen
gliders over dry bones,
captains of any tide,
bleached shell, or tooth.

Black flags, from the blue
they drop, sharp beaks
in strict formations,
shrieking pirates
ruffled feathers
storming ashore
on unseen ropes

cruising twilight breezes
over ratter tatter palms,
the flocks gather to land
all sizes, by rank, in order
as daylight cedes to darkness,

an endless rhythm
spins in the first sparkles
of early evening stars,
orange moon ascending,
a sun lingering still
in cinnamon billows,
feathery wisps above
white daylight slides
into a purple mix
not yet full dark

DANGEROUS WATERS

Other than gulls
nothing stands near
this edge of cold
endless water
we call home,
no matter the danger
beside me nearer
warmer, you.

FATHER

This week would be your birthday, no. 116.
How is it I speak to you so often still,
so many more times than before,
familiar conversations, so much to like
with little new to say?

Some times our meetings wander paths
with weathered signs -- where you come from,
who you are -- and then, the way of daydreams,
become dead ends with no direction out.

More promises, there, over the horizon
in the waves, rolling, hidden answers
tempting, impossible answers, hidden,
they swim for years in the heart.

No matter they raise their arms and call,
they are unreachable from this place here
where I wait in the dunes of longer nights
for signals struggling to see them by the dawn
rising always the same without my help.

FINDING A VOICE

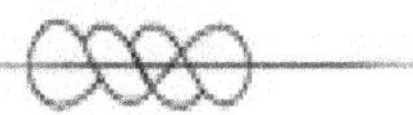

An act of juggling
many balls at once,
one me or another
in the air usually
for a moment in hand.

FLORIDA KEYS

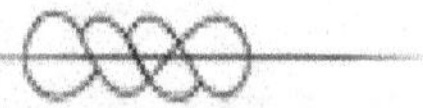

Yes, yes, sunlight, ripples,
currents, foam, tips of white caps,
the flop and flash of snapper on a feed,
the full squawk of gulls on a mission
winging deep into clouds, the white billows
of swans that float into dusk huge.

Yes too to sweet fragrances,
frangipanis, jasmine
on tiptoe close behind,
how things feel most of all,
the sinking hook of the sea,
singing beaks that strum the ribs
rhythms riding on the waves,
in the winds that ramble everywhere,
to flap in flags, splash into boats
as the sea rises, and we watch elephants
tread underwater island to island
from the secret still hidden porches
at the sundowner cafés of surprises.

HOW IT STARTED

I never heard mother's secrets,
not all,
who she was, or father,
why visits were so short.
She'd give my hand a squeeze
that silenced every question,
my fingers swallowed in her palm.

The hollow of her hand,
taught me everything,
spot the fishy, wild faces
sliding in from corners,
to blend, to slip away, to turn
her terror in all public places
into a pearl of safely in her palm.

Whatever light I wake to first,
when every road is blocked,
and I know I no longer know,
so firmly in the grip of doubt--
that is my terra firma,
first honkings of the wild geese,
poems taking wing from the comfort zone,
to far places of undiscovered secrets.

Tod Perry

I CAN FLY

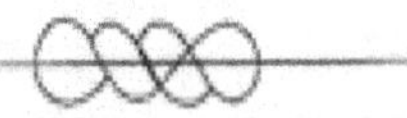

I can fly.
see into the past,
through most everything,
some things not at all.
speak at times for the unborn,
confer often with the dead.

I could never tell one
bad woman from the good
but learned all can bite.

I recall no useful words
for those I still love,
shielded no flower
against the cold.
There was a time I swam
under water 50 yards
and proved it twice.

I forgot nothing for years,
tinker with a line for 20 years
watch everything grow distant.
I cannot hold back time.
It seeps through fingers,
howls with the wind in my bones.

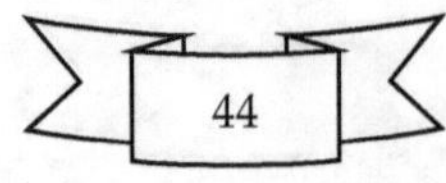

INDECISION

The temptation to do two things
opposite with undulating ardor,
wanting most the one and then the next
until it changes to the lesser other,
which after lightning bolt revisions
is once again the choice in greater favor.

So it goes this back and forth
as indecision mounts the steps
into an open door where compromise
beckons onward to another path,
where we abandon the either and the or,
both now, to an oncoming neither/nor,
a flip flopping third alternative,
a spontaneous fresh puppy, unwanted
but acting at home and now in the house.

Not considered from the start
the third becomes the first and last
and single option left on the table,
the only plan remembered over time,
that common thread that ties us to family
to home and in time to the acceptable,
tail wagging things we have become.
Meanwhile, outside, another door

keeps banging in the wind,
always banging, banging.

INTO THE DEEP

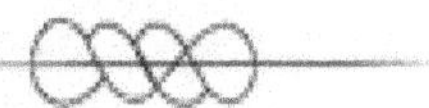

Born into war, to war re-borne,
new wounds shout to find a name:
new horrors heaped on the known,
bodies hanging raw as ragged seaweed
mixed into the odors of low tide and heat.

A burst, the thud into quiet,
who knows which flare was first into dawn—
the way first seconds can slow tick
in the mind and last a lifetime--
a sudden clap-- a bird becomes feathers,
a drifting array in the air,
fresh prey of a hawk, body split,
first blood spinning in the wind,
spinning past the farthest cliffs,
beyond the sharp edges of the end,
the flashing lighthouse, the clang of bells,
every sound diving into silence.

LANGUAGE

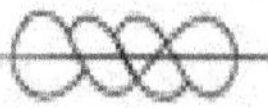

It flows on rivers music on air,
blood in history
long streams plunging
swiftly by mountains
to swirl through time

bays with hounds,
shoots through canyons,
its arrows curling
from ages of ice
recorded in stone.

We swim beside
on borrowed minutes,
swept up in a power,
of twisting sinews

opening our hearts
before it speaks
no more to us,
or in tongues only
before we go under
the oncoming wake
of a leviathan passing
to wilder stories beyond.

RUMPLESTILTSKIN SUMS UP THE DAY

A glass is always seen half full,
I'm told, I'm told,
even if it seems half empty,
or often even less maybe.

Mostly its the loudest people
who insist half full, or nearly full,
call me names and tell me to smile,
that blessings follow all in a while.

They say my struggles with this dilemma —
their close to full when I say empty —
brings only harm to my shaky kharma.
Time to check with Humpty Dumpty.

Tod Perry

SAND IN MY HOURGLASS

Olie, Olie, Olie,
home free ring-a-leaveo,
Georgie Porgie puddin n'pie
kissed the girls and made em cry,
Louis, Joe, and John L. too.

Spike Jones and Captain Marvel
ring around and Rosy gone
down that hole with puree marbles,
Columbo, Russ
and Ischkabibble.

Billy Rose and Arthur G,.
Guy Lombardo, old acquaintance,
Paul Whiteman, shall we dance?
Sour pickles in wooden barrels,
Buffalos first before buffalo nickels
liberty halves and silver dollars.

Bing was good, and Blue eyes too,
in them we trusted more than not,
vanished things so long forgotten.

The dunes once endless
far as forever, tips on the sky,

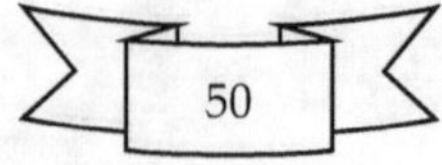

the sand is warm in my blue eyes,
glasses full until the last hour.

SEA DANCER

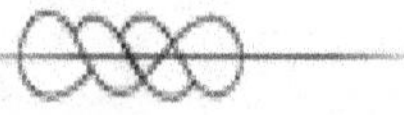

I survived the froth
summers of youth
scaled the surf,
swirling ballyhoo
in flight to sunlight
helter skelter
over waves swollen
King mackerel
in full chase.

In elusive dreams
wishes swim
in rolling oceans'
graceful waves
into darkness
trusting art.

While light still spins
wing crowded skies
with an early moon,
I dance this hour more
glide on the sea
the rain in my arms.

TSUNAMI

It took a shrug for the earth to tilt
for an ocean to spill from its floor;
then days only for survivors to stagger back,
scratch the ruins and start remaking yesterday.
We clearly lack a sense or any inner ear
to convince us how our towers turn to sand,
the sea washes everything to sea,
our clustered cities dart away
as schools of pin fish in a burst.
no scars have taught us where or what,
no memories how we ride the waves as ants
swept up on the tongue of God.

Instead we tidy up, pick at odds and ends,
pull on nets for threads of dazed survivors.
We count the dead and push the tides
with brooms. Though numb with fatigue,
motion is everything,
Knock us down, knock us around,
something sets us right
in every wrong direction.

Facing clouds of despair, we clearly see
how providence adorns our toils,
and blesses our transcendent spirit.

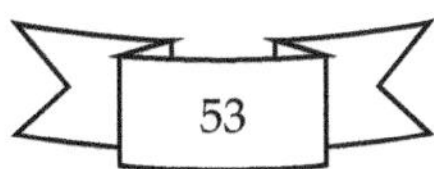

Against the burgeoning debris,
in the grasp of grief,
we slosh among the dead,
born again to take our chances by the sea,
as the fish that swim beside our nets.

VENTURE OUT

Aldi almost surely is looking over toward us
but cannot see inside our one way windows
from her stilt house just across the canal.
I can see you are watching Howard now,
outside upon a higher porch in the light,
shielding his eyes from the western sun,
staring somewhere on some lower level
cottage, like ours, but to the right,
at others on watch over there too.
From this angle I get the picture
each day we grow smaller,
inside a guarded bowl,
watchful as goldfish.

SECTION FOUR: LATE

NO TURNING BACK

As one who forgets not,
I cannot explain
love so deeply
buried under years.

How your signals
in plain sight
were hidden to me
yet circled back-

As faded memory
clear in the rings
at the core of a heart
where all the paths
twist back to you.

Tod Perry

A SIMPLE PIN

Loaded weapons
flags on lapels,
red faces shouting
US-A US-A,
angry Fox news
hot running words
mindless chickens
twisting all day
to corporate will,

to faith based laws
to flags on pins
smells of old money
from sea to sea
ending up boom boom
blood on the streets.

Sheep keeping faith
in fork-tongued myths
in gardens of anger
where fresh lies are spun
from tissues of truth,
and rebel flags wave
in slick masquerades
of a sham heritage

that withers the senses,
and seeps into bones.

Where zealots tote guns
and claim as their own
the valor marched home
by mixed generations.
A flag deeply stained
by double talk code
it hisses with danger
that snakes into life
sharp as a whip,
to show who has bite

and who sets the rules.
where elites in fresh jeans
dance with the toothless,
old Joe the plumber,
old ghosts of grey,
united in passions
seditions, revisions,
to past insurrections
linked by days, not so many,
back into time to the time.

Where air waves bellow
a rush of Sieg Heils,
goodbye old disguises,
hoods with white spikes,

Tod Perry

no burning of crosses,
a simple pin only,
the land of exceptions
salutes to the chosen,
the sons of the sons
of a new master race
a tribe at the heart
with lines in the sand
you never can cross
but worn on lapels

in white cowboy hats
they croon on tall horses
sad songs of tough love,
the high cost of freedom,
how hard it is earned
and paid for in blood
and never was free.

So sweet, so tasty
a land so cotton
so soft so candy,
it's lost on a tongue,
the promises glitter
and dance in the sky,
out there beyond us,
balloons with no strings
for hands reaching out
for the downward trickle

of windfalls once promised
and destined by birth.

A simple pin,
its roots crooked deep,
brings tears to the eyes
of the lost and confused
the more it divides —
this shackle with spikes
so stained with dark blood —
that cuts to the core
into chaos in chains,
to ghosts of lost wars
still biding their time
with old bones to pick.

Tod Perry

AGING IS A CONDOM

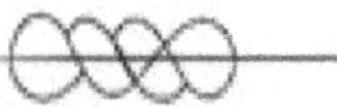

A condom slipper bony fingers
fit onto life until it matches
to cool the cries of gulls still calling
the meek to dance and tap flamenco.

A cap on desire, it slows what flows
from the wick, gushes to freedom from
the marrow in the wagging souls of men.

Lame birds, today they hop on stones,
along dry paths, graveyards of dreams,
on thirsty corners where small rain falls.

Where springs were fountains, clear once,
the fields are leaner, the streams entangled
with the faded beyonds that nag the heart,
the butterfly angels, the dancing wings.

In a winter coat on days too warm
and useless when surprised by cold,
Mr. Bojangles has tap in his toes still,
feet that shuffle through tingle and chill,
and a muffled music thick in the air.

BLACK SHEEP

The time has come to drop it,
just put away that unyielding script
written over months until
finally it's an overwritten puzzle
best kept out of sight inside a folder
with finished things that yet are not.

Put somewhere with unwanted gifts,
or tucked away with metal statues
of obscure heroes by time forgotten
inside the leafy corners of a park,
ignored, until come upon by chance.

A time eater from the first it plants
suggestions into awkward places,
shiny diversions into crowded spaces,
becomes the ever chatty neighbor
blocking every path back home.

Appearing first as inspiration,
his smile has charm, before
he strays in many headed-wrong directions,
and once in control becomes the show
stakes his all on his grander vision,
his better feeling for words on a page

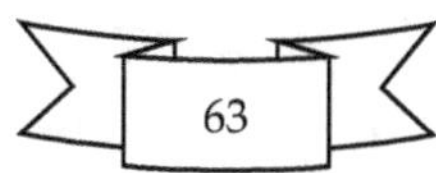

on any subject you thought was yours.
So quick to predict the first to quit,
he twists your words into pretzels, plus
now offers lessons on why you will lose.

Not a good winner no matter the end,
confidence high, he snickers boldly
as he nestles in at the top of that folder
growing thicker with distant cousins,
youngest in a mob of black sheep,
and so like the rest of the family

CORKSCREW

He walks to his room
down a hall sees
himself in himself
smaller smaller
mirror in mirror
unsure what image
in which mirror he is.

Shows in that moment
by a pace that slows
him worn by distractions
from the weight of his day,

Sinks down into bed
first left
then right
spins into darkness
that turns into dawn,
and in one final whirl,
twists himself up,
upright, erect.

Tod Perry

CRAZY DONNIE,
COMMANDER OF GUAM

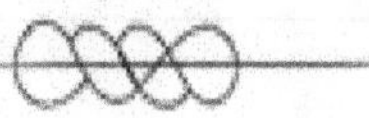

A Commander suddenly
of a pacific island,
21 years old,
and by default
the one-day ruler
of all things Guam.

All the food too,
under His command, ranking
Executive C. O.,
the sun and king
Ensign Crazy Donnie.

Shit happens.

Guam, an island
atop a sea of fish,
had plenty of people
fighting through hunger
but no boats in the water
to keep the old ways alive
and under a sun they all knew.

In Donnie sailed with his ulcer,

a ray of light on a cargo ship
from a grand victorious fleet
with luck and great power to pity
plus a shipload of American cheese.

A food with an odor as strong as bait,
not for the eating and who could trust
a melting gift that smells of death
before a piece goes down the throat.

Donnie had a stomach for this tale of cheese
and another one about dodo birds,
too dumb to eat white bread, too clumsy
to get off runways to avoid extinction.

Tod Perry

CRAZY DONNIE CROSSES THE LINE

In the Babe's own hand! The great
Babe Ruth! Donnie yanked out
his draft card, his anything
to get that signature
for the kid at home (the one
he called little brother),
who took no time to lose it,

who saw no magic in hang dog jowls
longer than a basset's face,
who knew baggy pants are only worn
by men already old, like golfers.

Older than Joe DiMaggio,
chasing fly balls all summer
with no excuses for his flaming spurs
in the bones of his famous heels.
Joltin Joe, 17 homers only
by the final day of July.

Joe scribbled his greetings too,
once cornered and no way to escape
from half deaf Crazy Donnie
and his shifty mixtures of craft
thickened with plenty of crazy.

Old Town Clown

Swift as a bolt came a voice from within,
the spirit of a bolder Donnie sprang out
free from the walls of an adult skin
to spin a tale of a kid sick at home
full of need and high hopes and dreams
to honor Joe's name as a trophy of ink,
so he snatched a pen it seemed from the air,
and by magic made the dream in his hands.

That card went AWOL too, it slipped somewhere
away and soon was forgotten until
suddenly found in a flea market bin
dragged out of the past like magic from dust,
and letter by letter came back to the present.

Easy lost, easy stolen,
given away, taken back
one act fits inside the other,
roots can tie, roots can tear.
A single navel, a common blood,
fickle time thickens or dilutes.
Gifts shared and given freely
get taken again and kept in secret,
with guilt at first then later style.

Poison gifts are gifts from life
sharp elbows of its sharp equations
that crouch inside the poisoned heart,
and spread through genes inside our blood,

what calculates what divides, what dies
when brother takes away from brother,
what crowns the man with craft a king
whose stolen gifts felt once ill gotten
but stolen twice feels all forgotten.

CRAZY DONNIE DOES LAS VEGAS

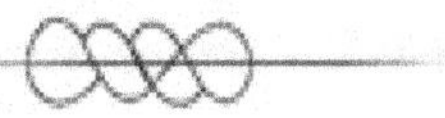

The kid's a zillionaire,
loose money in bundles
squirts free from his pockets
as he rampages all night on a tear.

Not once to the amazement
of whole bar rooms gazing,
does he spill when he tilts,
this great pumpkin on stilts,
or drop when he stumbles,
not quick stepping Donnie
the zillionaire kid.

Mumbling and bumbling,
most see he's absurd,
just an old fashion goof,
but with hopes undeterred,
bounces one way, then this way,
hanging in, hanging tall,
quick stepping, a hoofer
out of phase with it all.

High hopes for a howl,
he goes West for the fun
for guitars and sun,

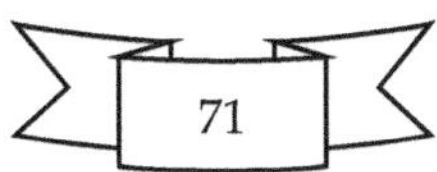

the last time maybe
before it's all over
to find dreams in his bankroll
leaping green from a fishbowl
where gold lasts forever,
and he dances in clover.

CRAZY DONNIE FRESH FROM WAR

Back in the home town fresh from war
so long away and not one wound.
Ensign Donnie, the family star, a vet
the city honors with all the names
now chiseled deep into slabs of marble.

Yet everywhere, this loud hatred of Harry.
With a stroke to the fuzz on his chin, Donnie said
how time would be kinder to Harry S,
would rank him high, but below FDR,
who was hated even more than HST.

Hard to figure such hate from thin air,
in all the news, coming so soon
after war over hatred was only just won,
and almost won against hunger too.

Which brings us in closer to Donnie's world
of confusing places so full of raw hunger,
and people begging for something to eat.

The three of us listened, confused by his visions,
each story full of mean contradictions.
Me, my sister and Buddy, our dog,
when Donnie said hunger will do even more,

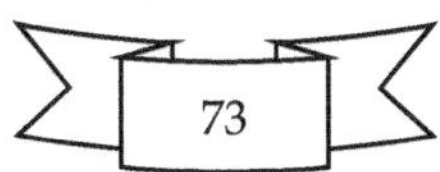

we'd eat our own Buddy in certain conditions,
a lesson we knew could never come true.

Yes eat him, he said, gently stroking the fur
inside Buddy's soft ears. Unthinkable thought,
we fought it like hunger, and yet we considered,
could love of our Buddy be so silly, so shallow?

We learned Donnie's crazy, and not always nice,
but what did we know, as he got to his point—
that life is a game, you might lose your stake,
the person you started out first to become
may not be the same to come home in the end.

CRAZY DONNIE MARCHES DOWNFIELD

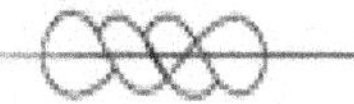

Donnie and his shiny tuba
marched downfield half times,
saw Notre Dame football free
then confessed
he couldn't play
his tuba even.
No one noticed
his ulcer either, how deaf
& batshit crazy on his way
to graduation, a US Navy
commission, then back from war
took over the family
business, fired dad,
kick-stepping straight
down silver paths,
golden-domed tomorrows.

Tod Perry

CRAZY DONNIE'S NEW LIFE

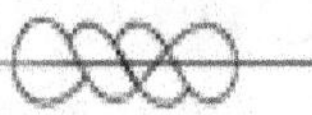

Crazy Donnie sent
mother love letters
travelling long
roads lone places
like Texas lost
drunk forgot
posted them.

Another time
pretending sleep
zombie walked in-
to sister's room
no pretending
intent. Anyone
knew him not
surprised one bit.

Not that crazy,
fox bit himself
free of the life
he knew, knew him
to start anew,
got rich, distant,
stopped writing
friends and family

never in doubt
he'll come about

Tod Perry

DISTURBING THE PRESENT

The future stands before us, clear
on the path, no need for stars to guide
with its lanterns through these trellises
of visible darkness into which we slide,

sand into minutes, days of protracted worry,
where unforgiven deeds catch with hooks
what squirms in the rocks of our dreams,
scurries always below
the steadiest hand
and a watch ticking
into endless overtimes,
all anchored in the wreckage of events
long past, skeletons sunken,
by wounds too deep,
where big fish from the past
swim fresh into the present.

FACEBOOK

I've got to take my name off Facebook.
My page opens to sad eyes, long faces
of dogs, of cats, the pampered loves
so darling to my expanded family,
the dogs and cats of all their friends,
and all threatened creatures in the world.

Tigers and horses are not off limits.
Calls to rescue every coddled pet
in danger fill up my daily pages
with expressions of enduring love.
The eyes of predators inspire pleas
for adoption, for stays of execution,
then endless likes and passionate loves
past borders, into realms of devotion.

Well, certainly into adoration,
edging closer to reverence,
and core belief for certain cults:
our pets have souls, and even more,
when the sun sets finally on their days,
their spirits rise straight up to heaven.

With deep respect for dogs, all those
in emotional service, the most feral beast,

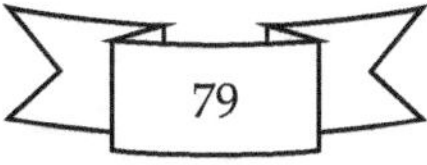

somehow each one worthy of salvation,
but dare I protest somewhere in safety
the posts of praises, the daily altars
with cards of sympathy and tearful poems,
the final gifts of French champagnes?

Such tributes pain me when I realize
the tenderness is real. It pours out freely,
even opens doors to total strangers,
and shows my heart is doomed to wander
in a world where love arrives too often late
on postcards, or blizzards of disappearances,
how tears are shed for those who live forever,
so few for beggars or their ragged souls.

HURRICANE IRMA

SEA
Our hearts are closest to the sea
study the smallest details
of this first among all loves,
reaching for any spaces near it.
A heart that reads the sea
sees fact in all its warnings.

The mind just settles anywhere,
never near enough to the sea,
where it calculates the invisible,
the quickness of wind, its sudden
lift and the rise to authority.

Though wind and the sea collude,
no mind can read wind. In one blow
it sweeps in unseen, clean.
We go down all injured somehow.

WIND
Wind reveals next to nothing,
dances little dances, confounds,
holds secrets tight, cavorts
hand in hand with the sea,
confiding everything, and often

as they want, but not with you.

Our minds see nothing of the wind
with one eye fixed on the sea,
the wind is quicker than one eye,
one swipe of a claw you won't see.

The mind is a toy in the wind
as it hides and changes faces
much too fast for any plan.

Ignored, a sea will eat the heart
alive; wind is a cat paw
to any trust, a mad surgeon,
reveling, on the ready
to strip bone to the white,
one slice of downdraft, suddenly
wind is a spinning scalpel.

KATHY'S SHADOW

Pieces fly first
whole chunks later
parts that matter,
a shadow leaning
away; then after,
everything matters
by its absence.

My younger sister
gone, a presence
beside me always
there in my trust
hardly noticed
till suddenly not.

Her loss is absence
of always behind
then just ahead,
her death a vapor
of nothing left
when all is lost.

Nothing yet convinces me
she will not tag along,
that I will not protect her,

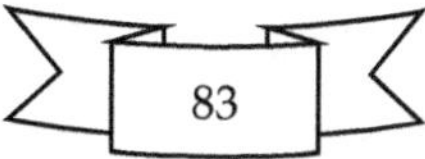

which was, when all is said,
my only job from the start.

The winner here is loss
on steps at ugly angles,
crooked death by my door,
a ghost more likely lost
while on its way for me.

Good night dear tag along,
your memory is my torch now,
and you, so long the keeper
 of the flame and all the freckles
of a family that grew up once
in a house by an edge of the sea.

That torch has fallen to my hands,
the last, I hold on tighter now
so others know your warmth,
in this smoldering finality
your light flickers in embers,
in moods among shadows
inside me deep to the end.

LINDOS, GREECE

In layers white walls climb inside white walls,
rose of Lindos, it blooms above green
Mediterranean waters, petals unfolding
in spirals high into Hellenic blue.

Through narrow turns on crooked ways,
wild donkeys wander beside stray goats,
the same that crossed the paths of gods
who strolled these narrow stones for hours
and dawdled under skies as blue today.

By dark, the tavernas on the rooftops glow.
Buzzing beehives, they frame the night
warm laughter humming down the paths
where strangers hug with strangers, kiss,
then pose for any camera blinking red,
random flashes in forgotten moments
pasted, and forever lost in album pages.

In the later hours, as evening withers,
but hope stays strong, still on its feet,
a voice could challenge you to follow
against your instinct down hidden lanes
to seek what calls out in your dreams,
a hideaway alley to an inner dawn

that opens late in life to beauty
its fresh promises on full wings
cutting paths deep into old stone.

MCTURTLE'S CHIN

Horns on horns
a deadly din
the ass of Manhattan
brays from his tower
trumpets untruth
the braggart therein
in all things uncouth
and somewhere south in McTurtle's chin

He's angry and crazy
with lies quick and sleazy
double-backed words
that reek of Putin,
a bloated twit lacking wit,
nothing civil or just,
just an odor of worse
from the rest of the stuff down McTurtle's chin.

No room here for facts
even worse for ideas,
the stones of our values
erode and grow thin
quickly turning to sand,
all gone with no comment
and sink to the deep of McTurtle's chin.

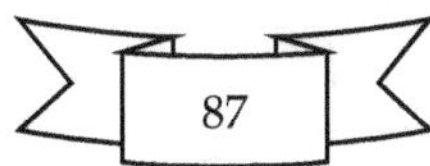

The truth we saw coming,
what blazed from his eyes
only showed we are blind
to the power of lies,
for we knew even then
this sack full of skin
so chock full of kin
had more of that stuff down McTurtle's chin.

We heard his crass humor
and gagged through the spring,
but thought OK then,
a short little spin,
just boasts from this sewer
and soon after summer
our relief would be golden
not piss from hyenas down McTurtle's chin.

OLD TOWN CLOWN

Thrilled to be the scruffy clown
his clothes were blots on polka dots
on top of rings on top of spots
paint in drips from collar to cuff
half a Pollack half a Matisse.

The splotches put bounce in his local fame
and soothed his downward drifting soul,
an aura of blooms, of something foaming,
snowy gusts or butterflies dancing.

For a town confused by the image it crafted
a perfect canvas to fit paradise,
its visible emperor in floating clothes,
and the dotted king of a dotty life.

But when he awoke still caked in paint,
the aura deflated. He had no work,
unless in the wakes of Eden's storms,
the Wilmas and Georges he barely survived
by scraping on mold while dangling nauseous
on the tops of hot roofs to hang on to tin,
his soul turned to toast overcooked in a heat,
that shot in his shoes like nails made of fire.

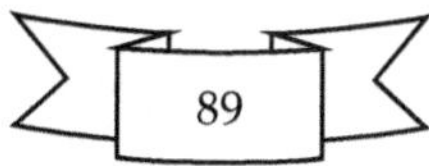

Tod Perry

All work was a swelter, but mostly he crawled
upside down under double wides by inches
his body lathered in a boil of sweat
his eyes on alert and strained with a fear
of things that spring in darkened spaces.

On such a day a notion took flight, the wing
of a turkey buzzard straight from the clouds
and for him a fresh wind into Eden,
the day when steam rose up from his skin,
came out of his shirt in visible puffs.

No more for him the laid back frog
doomed to nestle and cook in a pot,
a servant to servers for pocket coins.
Time to strike his new path had come,
old town spots for new town stripes,
the resolve to quit what doesn't pay
just boiled up, iced tea, no sugar.

On an island open to any hustle
the time had come to change his act,
to wear fresh clothes, and so appear
to fix his brand with smoke and mirrors
pin wings on his caterpillar friends
and let them fly around the clock.

He thrives by mixing art and business,
books small losses, files taxes,

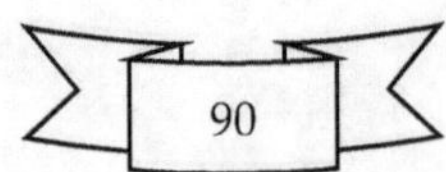

has a home on any stool down under,
a lucky muse who helps his rise.
He hands out business cards that read:
"Driftwood Crafts + Management,"
and so combines all work with play,
chats with clients at special socials
and other events on several phones
when he arrives by SUV.

He deals with drifters heading home late,
and many more on their way at dawn,
moves mostly alone in dark off hours
an invisible ship that roams the night.
He might lift anchor unexpectedly,
his Jolly Roger aloft in the sky,
balls of powder, feathery puffs,
dandelions drifting high in the clouds,
white thunder straight up to heaven.

Tod Perry

ONCE A CLAMDIGGER

Away from the city, the job and the wars,
I wade in the wetlands of Great South Bay
knee high in muck, half hidden by weeds,
white as the herons that make this marsh home
roaming a deep low tide of the early morning.

Not far the seagulls eye me from a strip of sand.
I hear them jostle, the peevish flapping of their wings,
their calls that echo how this bar is theirs, all theirs,
but I was born by this same bay, with some rights too,
and I can stand for hours on my own reedy legs.

Some inner tide drags me here, back home,
where long dead roots stab hard into my feet,
where scallops shake and chatter in my hands.
It tugs me into shallows thick with broken shells,
and spiky crabs, their pincers raised, and ready
to pick a fight or challenge toes to stand.

Wading deeper in the mud, the cooler layers soothe,
oozing up between the toes, while my soul,
or else its ghost, sinks down into my feet, lured
by lullabies of swamp and tides, and then takes root,
sprouting outward from my toenails, shining
one by one, black and fresh as cherry stones.

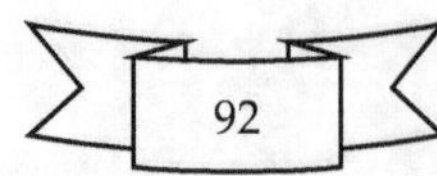

ONE WAY TICKET

Handmade Persian rugs, a family craft
for generations, signatures treasured
worldwide as a way of life
for clans with their distinct voices
woven in like a chorus of angels.

Whatever the origins of this art,
it's no way now to make a living.
The work is hard, just as a pearl
is for an oyster, takes too much time,
and there's no profit in it any more,
unless for certain men from the shadows
in time of need with clever calculation,
to shield grey assets from probing eyes
can tuck this value into cheap collections,
like cash under the rug so to say,
made harder to price than currency
rolled tight, all packed and sealed
and ready to be shipped in haste.

How much better this fate seems
than other arts that hit the skids.
A poem is purchased for a song,
a good one for a lucky penny,
and who knows what a Haiku brings?

Tod Perry

Even simple things once useful
hold on to value after. Wooden shoes,
once worn, were later good for sabotage,
and sell now as kitsch on corners--that,
or nailed to walls for decoration.
A horse no longer works the farm so hard,
poses less in paintings yet stays a horse.
Old singers of the blues who hardly stand,
will sing for tips, then hang around like moss
that lingers from a nether world, until,
in their legend late, they hit some green.

Some truth lies just below the surface
hidden where it does less harm.
Those women, like those who stirred my fires
years ago, can take my breath today.
Though music changes rhythms, music it remains,
new actors bring a role to life on stages
as others gave it breath in other ages.

Some things about our lives grow dry,
pieces for museums set under glass,
or else become an odd acquired taste,
like reading Latin just for fun,
the scale of its heroic fables
hurtling down pages by syllables,
alive today as wild caught fish,
or white tigers in the melting snows,
magicians in their tall black hats

who made things disappear on stages
then disappeared so well themselves.

Poetry is in these spaces, everywhere
with its sweet or sour gratifications
more lost at sea than Atlantis.
It wins no prize of hammered gold
no awards of lapis lazuli, not even
a one way ticket to modern Dogtown.
An unexpected trip to Byzantium,
its markets teem with greener parrots,
hot blooded dancers, crystal, cold
bony fish in the crowded throats of herons.

Tod Perry

PRECIOUS COINS

(In Memory: Dee, Dick, Don, and Mark)

Like music. memories of them cling,
the poets alive now in my ears
their voices ringing all in chorus
each one his song a candle flicker
so bright today yet once obscure.

Dee found poetry in everything
could see it growing from the ground
to flow inside us before we spit it
back again as seed into the wind.

Dick put every gear into forward
had juicy fame between his teeth
before it trickled back to earth
his blood rushed early into soil
teasing death on a motorcycle.

Don saw things before we did,
So far apart but always first
he dropped fresh crumbs for anyone
in search of art and shared his thirst.

Elegant and tall, Mark,
he truly was a friend,

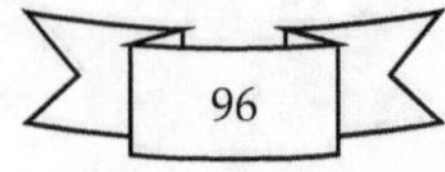

who never could imagine
just how to be a friend.

His had a natural grace,
a gravity and strange ideas
that roamed like weightless boulders
riding in from his outer space.

So when he said "you're close,"
that could be, or maybe so;
"not near enough that
so it all lets go". Right

there mark, so shrewd
so we can meet forgotten selves
and open doors to buried places.

Thanks Mark for that and plenty more.
No one plans to say goodbye,
we shared good wishes all for all
took small bits from one another,
in little bites that made us better.

Why then do I sometimes hear,
"OK, that's fine-- why then
are you not famous, at least
more like these famous friends?"

I say what matters, matters.

Tod Perry

Few poems bring poets fame
and yet become the blood and tea
for those who need their pints
to fertilize obscurity,

Most beauty dies soon as it's forged,
loose sand that slips into the strata,
its bloom in shadows trapped by time,
its radiance and glow gone dim
in blends of greys and beauty lost.

Who knows if treasure hides below,
and shines still naked as the day it's born,
how long it stands alone, —the if
or when it might be found in pieces
beneath our noses on the ground
with broken bones and arrowheads,
beside tin ears what precious coin?

QUE GUAPO

In these photos there are voices
saying what they said,
you just can't hear them.
None with the face in the mirror,
that demeanor of a nasty camel,
a Yasser Arafat in his later years.

At five, a smile radiates, dimple-blessed
with love straight from a mother's heart,
teeth wide apart and a still disarming
innocence in this buck-toothed beauty.

With my sister at ten with four hands each
counting the gloves pinned to our cuffs,
we're shoulder high in snow after a romp.
Scribbled on the border, "I loved that coat,"
that toothy boy with no idea of time
how close his hour to knuckle down.
I don't remember what was special
about the coat or why I loved it so.

We save old photos for our reasons,
I always hated them: too toothy
too thin, too much like my father.
I didn't know back then to calculate

how a lifetime starts with steps
all so alike till time deceives
and changes memory by degrees,
trusting powers I held within
to choose what things would stick,
what face would hold a hidden smile
still safe inside and fresh as yesterday.

"Que Guapo", the technician from Columbia says
(to my picture as a slender lad in white),
as she measures golden stumps in my gums,
white shirt, white pants, white shoes,
all 140 pounds, yes, 19 and handsome,
a day remembered for its ugly hangover;
the photo doesn't speak of the fuzzy head,
the lean stomach that growled from beer.

Que Guapo, so sincere, she means to compliment,
Que Sorpriso! In her eyes dressed so fine,
but suited in mine in working whites,
not a bit the well groomed caballero.
A camel harnessed for burdens, no time
for other liberating euphonies,
or any pleasures not foaming in a glass.
Awakened here, Que Guapo. The animal
alert to sounds and the scents of caravans,
at the start of a marathon to run full gallop.

Of these matters photos cannot speak,

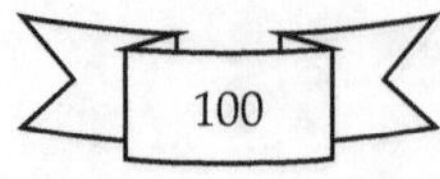

forgot to say, or never knew to say.
In nameless clusters the familiar fades
lost islands pasted in an album,
stranded messages, weak signals, dots and dashes
to a world now chattering in busy stacatto
with cyber-friends in terabytes and holograms.

Then time's distortions added more,
small and simple things began to fly,
the keys to start and soon the glasses,
new words and names of friends long gone,
wallet sections for cards and currencies,
IDs, and puzzling user names,
PINs, and passwords with daily alterations
in cybervaults with codes and keys,
some 48 and counting, or maybe 50 now
just like the states, (and some territories).
And so, the simple thoughts are buried,
important to start, but in the end unsaved.

That girl, who loved monkeys and the color purple
is a doctor now, or several kinds;
she fought through life for funds to save
the abandoned orphans that flood the earth.
Despite the heartaches of her work
that crushing world she hoped to shape,
she mourns, by Skype, for missing children
and not her fortunes lost for causes,
loves monkeys still and the color purple.

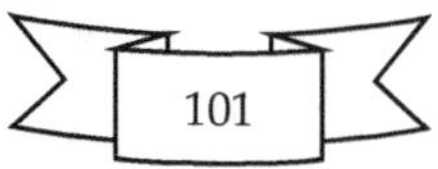

Tod Perry

What memories pale each day
are more than just a favorite coat:
the people first by ones, then groups
until whole buildings disappear.
The photos put a face on these,
a time and place to show what was,
a space to feel the forgotten rain
before the deluge when time spilled over
to well up in me here in this mirror,
at home on a path to somewhere
cozy and loud as a camel in the rain,
in a mix of things uncomfortable,
still on the road, still Que Guapo.

RUNAWAY HEART

Our eyes see things through the heart.
Nothing too plain for wide eyed revelation,
too lost our dreams cannot embrace them.
They rise before us in fresher colors,
in plumery, aromas, or more real
as though we never were alone.

Like vines our fingers reach up in air
as dancers touch their music with the feet,
so things sense things ready to happen,
though nothing touches, we see it all.

Some live for love, and yet outside,
life becoming much like love,
two curling question marks,
one fit snug inside the other,
each fused into a single dream
until they don't--there
once but not there now.

Sometimes, before a word is found,
the heart -- alive, new and green
parades across the dunes,
a graceful, forgetful flame
sweeping clean the tracks

of all it knows.

To the last we hold on tight
to things beyond all reasons,
and dance in sands enchanted,
aroused by perfumes,
ribbons of blue skies,
memories made new
from start to end.

SOMETHING IN THEM LOVES A WALL

Oh Arab Spring
before heads roll
Oh Orange revolution
buckets full of blood
Oh revolution of the Roses,
subversive blooms and grasses.
Set upon by arrows, the huddled 1%,
scented with fear in circled wagons.

Patience! That all things come full circle,
the spinning earth will tilt again.
What's right is in our laws unwritten.

Our justice cannot bear such wounds,
old wealth has needs, and seeks new gains,
to make new rules once back in charge,
vigor renewed, be ready to resolve
the endless problems of the poor,
those dripping heads inside of caskets.

There will be time for singing praises,
to heap full honors on the herded poor,
the chosen heroes of our modern wars,
first to die for flag and cross.
Champions ever for any cause

they march off proudly with heady grins,
cherished medals on swelling chests
to the thumpety thump de thump of tubas
uplifted by the praise they reap
for grit and sacrifices yet to come,
for the many pins that glitter brighter
than the youthful treasure of their lives.

How soon the glory of their wounds
like flowers wilt, forgotten before
the pains are suffered full, so soon
their lives surrendered won or lost
to honored crypts and final bugles.
Sacred once, they gather everywhere
like ghosts in rags, how poor these poor
outside the gates, now near the walls
built never tall nor strong enough
to keep these ragged out of sight.

Safe, but never quite invisible,
the wealthy hide inside safe walls,
the wicked rich in baseball caps,
designer trucks, in love with guns,
so bonded by entitlement, they gaze—
empty eyes behind electronic eyes
at the angry face of an angry stomach,--
growing plump with full resentment.

With animal spirits revived

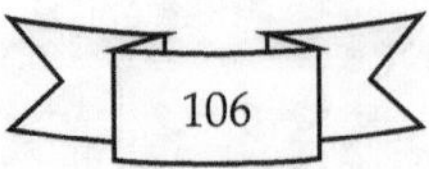

they lobby for greater shares,
for more of everything,
new funds new walls, and laws
to make the tough laws stricter.
And now they pray and pay
their God to tolerate them more,
a God more like them day by day.

With religion hard as bricks
they seek new ways to keep
the castles in their Eden safe,
to live in the graceful pink
of privacy and out of sight,
to choose just where and when
who will be roasted
without a squeal,
in isolation
or in the streets,
to prove for now
that once upon a time
there were no guillotines.
Something in them loves these walls.

Tod Perry

THANK YOU. NOW GOODBYE

She don't love me
but wants me around.
I don't own her
but wants me around
cause she owns me.

I can go somewhere else
cause she don't need me
but she wants me around.
++
I take everything from her,
she'll kill to protect me
12 wasps before breakfast
count at night each pill,
to keep me alive.
+++
Her melancholy goes deep,
a well of hurts long held within,
a shallow pool from some abuse
before the henna in her hair.
+
It's not the sadness I adore,
but an aura, even grace
so clear to this believer
her outstretched arms

the charm that rings her face
like saints in stained glass.
+++
Sunlight inside of mist,
untouchable rainbows,
thunder in blue air,
the music of leaves,
wings passing,
cold waves cracking
at the peak of winter.
+
It's not the sadness, no,
but how love surrounds
this swan with petals
at peace all alone
double in reflection
+++
Thank you. Now goodbye.

Tod Perry

THE SOUND OF THE WIND

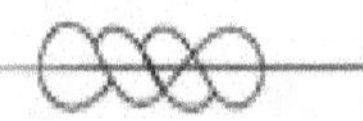

The hiss in the riggings
puts a fear in the ear
for men on the waves
not there for a man
who combs the shore.

For men at sea
when it bristles with spray,
the hackles it raises,
the thunderous sounds
that boom in the heart,
too close on their way
they batter the boy
still there in the man.

For those on the shore
when winds start their whirling
turning dunes into whipsaws
they wrestle great waves onto land,
crabs to dance in our gardens
lift islands lost long in their beds
black tar that sparkles in sunlight
and hints of more treasures
on top of the waves
on the way soon.

TOM THE FRIDGE

My new fridge has more than a few sharp words
on put down jokes, people called dumb, dumb
refrigerators, thick old white machines,
dumb in dumb out. My recent model mutters
like a nutty professor about how sleek his brain is,
how it has more in reserve, a sharper memory,
and better days ahead than some by far.

It mumbles this then goes about its chores,
doing things better each year with the quiet whirr
of a precise, electronically tuned Ferrari,
the background hum a gentle warning only
as I wander in the dark of night, beneficial
for what ails me-- a courtesy to my age.

So cool and smooth, Tom keeps me on my toes
when he adds, how much easier this might be
had he said nothing more, simply noted
how like us to never once consider fully
the better promise in his future plans
(including what happens in the kitchen at night,
the spot lit shadow of a skater alone on the ice,
whirling, in a sweat, and closing on perfection).

My fridge and I are getting closer too.

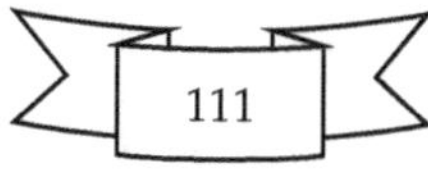

Tom's making calculations, even now I think,
about what's healthy and what to throw away,
whether we stashed aside enough for today,
checking what needs checking for the future.

No sense arguing there. Besides, down deep
this thing with fridge could turn out for the best,
a trend Tom sees promised by each new model. Maybe
"dumb fridge" might not be so bad a tag.
Just today Tom said I'd keep another day,
I'm not the worst, not so bad an egg at all.

UNLESS THINGS CHANGE

Unless things change at the tap
this one looks like the last poem.
Closing time is coming soon,
and I am stuck deep down a hole
in a shallow pond of drowning fish.

So long ago I learned that beauty
is truth, and truth beauty,
but from this end of the bar
the stools are looking last call empty
with beauty no longer sitting near.

My drink's gone sour. It's pants on fire,
the orange liar, who turns me into Cicero
no more the mild mannered poet,
I fiddle words, a loud mouth Nero
howling madly over flaming truth.

What force could stir me into action?
Dead babies? They wash ashore ignored
where truth was born in Greece, that passed
the orphaned gift onto a world of evil,
ancient mother of things sane and civil.

By closing time the joke's on me.

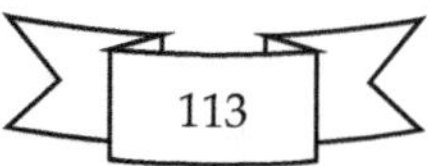

My truthy ardor is always dandy,
so close to beauty it seems to be,
warm light to show how others care
with kindness more than sugar candy.

I simply have no more ideas,
no quick solutions, no explanations.
The glass looks empty, no more poems.
To change the liar change the beer.
Top it up love, give it time so it foams.

WHEN COWS COME HOME

For no clear reason I keep waiting
for the cows to come home, words
my father used for plans usually
too reckless to be realized,
less likely than shrimp to whistle.

It mattered little how cows have relied
on returning home without fail, clanging
the whole way down from the hills, always,
but for my father, and for me, those cows
could end up anywhere, just not back home.

His words stick inside my head,
his spirit races in my blood
when I reach for elusive truths,
or search for better things beyond
the simple answers close at hand
within my reach and easy to grasp.

Over the green fields of the Fulda Gap,
speeding home on the fleet Deutsche Bahn,
as it rolls toward evening, fields full
of all those cows that should be home.

They look relaxed, lounging for now

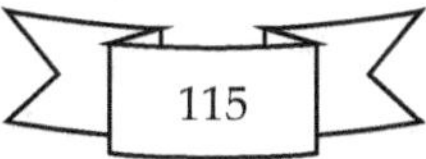

in the lingering light of summer to gaze
at flashes of light off a silver train streaking
from one ripe valley and on to another--

me inside, in a hurry, chapped lips,
sore feet in need of a stretch,
on my way home back to warmth,
a dinner delayed and some worries
that grew in my time afield.

More and more these cows in their idle
look like my plans, the wobbly ones
that stand in place for no reasons, idle,
no urge to move from here to there,
not now, not later. Never seems a good time
for any kind of change, they all suggest.

They could be on to something true and simple
at the heart of a fading season, an inner bell
that rings at one exact time, clearly
so I hear it too, that recognizes when
to stop the wandering, think more of things
with answers, about the coming weather,
and when it's right to come inside.

YOU MAKE THE MONKEY

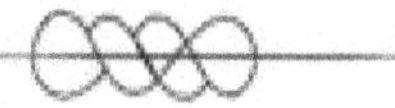

The second I see you
the monkey in me mambos,
a force that turned the weed
of youth into a sinew
then spread into a canopy
full green with chatter
the rustling tides of wind
you hear in the leaves
on calm days too.

But closer now,
another rhythm, yours,
songs you carried to our tree
darting in and out each day
and foreign as a belly dancer.
Wasn't that your plan all along,
the moment the music you are
woke the monkey in my heart?

YOUR GARDEN

Short visits expected
in her garden
I'm sent off quickly
banished elsewhere,
upstairs where
clothes on a chair
are laid out fresh
pressed and folded,
slippers below.

My visit is welcomed
more than a wasp,
not so much
as a bumble bee,

With a nod to politeness,
a trace of distraction
the smile fades.
I'm waved off, or
waved at.

It's love, some tell me
to think hydrangea,
last year pink ones,
this season bursting
new changes all blue.

SECTION FIVE:
NEW POEMS, 2023

A RAGGEDY TOY

In rags an old toy
dumped in a washer
out it comes clean
feeling now fresher
back on the scene,
a new man for sure
still clever your boy
as cool as a Porsche

Tod Perry

COMING OF AGE AGAIN

One clumsy stumble, and presto, the roles reverse,
another misstep is added to my children's fears,
their words growing sweet with kindnesses,
and all deflected with guile and sly resistance.

No matter what heights or the towers I leap,
the tallest buildings, yes, on sheepish feet,
they see only age, a gray nose in the tent,
a heart that soldiers on with a dodgy skip,
those shaky legs are just another hint.

Time can wait years but catches every fox,
one careless moment is startled by sharp facts,
a flash with stings of instant revelation
when endless paths meet an unexpected end.

With no Plan B, nor optional life style off ramps,
from here it's one way forward, off to nowhere
flat feet, hard ground, one body with some lumps,
lost in its wrinkled clothes it feeds on dreams-
Balloons float there grinning in the twilight air.

CRABS IN KETTLES

Master of snarls,
inscrutable cords
to bamboo blinds
let sea smells in,
the breath of the sea
let it in, let it in
to smell you air out.

Quick handed snatcher
master crab catcher
a once dead-eye netter
of blue sea skimmers,
slick sideways swimmers
with translucent flippers
and razor sharp nippers

Blue eyes dawdles there
in the long ago still
in that dream back then
time scratched the skies,
leaves above chimed
when winds stretched forever
as a breeze under trees

Claws scrambling in kettles

pots rattle, pots tumble
dinner scratching metal
those hot boiling claws
he eats with his paws
and bites with his jaws

DUMPTEE TELLS ALL

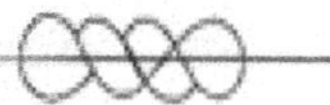

Dumptee Trumptee shat on this wall,

said beautiful, perfect, powerful tall,

get set he tweeted, for a strong win next fall,

when down comes this virus shat out of control,

Mexicans, Alamo storming, shat in free fall,

a crooked DEM hoax, a fake media call,

Dumptee retweeted, then could not recall

one fall, or ever he shat one wall or all.

Tod Perry

EMPEROR OF CHAOS

One hand claps, or whistles whatever
so says the mobster, a walker on water
narcissist colossus whose vicious trick
is promises fading from later to never.

Words bent to ugly that stick as a rumor
at first unlikely they twist into probables,
then storms from a pulpit quick as a tumor
catnip for mobs of fanatics and troubles.

Some pirates are known to don their own halos,
but aboard this ark, he's the admiral of sleeze,
a clown with a crown who whines in disguise —
the king rat upon us, the conman who owns you,
a heart without soul down a throat full of lies.

At rallies he gloats and floats on false pride
and wallows in oceans of alternate facts.
Fools gold is his hair, a prop like a wig,
in suits fit for whales, red ties for the pig
who utters more trash and snark to alarm
cheers to cheap shots mixing louder and wide
while Proud Boys stand by still hatching attacks
the captain of chaos tied fast to the helm.

FALLING

A leaf falling
spinning down early
green to ground.
No need to turn
red or brown
it feels a calling,

Week over week,
faithfully calling,
remembering a Spring,
one last like the first,
you asking then
did I notice lately
how much we forget?

This recent spring you
your spin just begun.
I'll never forget
or bury what ends
as moments of silence
both ends of the phone.

Before leaf hits ground,
to curl into absence,
wide eyes grown wet

Tod Perry

one hand stretches out
to catch the knives falling
a careless heart missed
every chance long gone.

GRAVITY

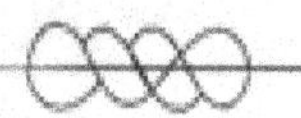

The moon will lift the oceans
across the face of the earth
its urges turning tides
to waves of foaming surf.

Above a mountain range
a silver crescent, yet full,
a pumpkin huge and orange.

Commander of seven seas,
it rules our hearts in a voice
with roots inside our genes.

Lovers speak its language,
what bodies simply know
moonstruck at any age.

In altering shapes and shades,
a slender blade in winter,
in tropical red, full blood,
it reaches in to touch us
this gravity we call love.

Tod Perry

GUINEOS MANZANOS
(APPLE BANANAS)

Apples always down to the core, no worries,
from apple branches dropped, and still today,
no wisps in the air of blossoms from banana trees.

New times, new facts, and thanks to DNA
some questions ripen on the roots of stories.

In family photos those spectral faces, for years
so safely kept, and some perhaps with tears,
were these just nameless grains, forgotten sands,
the nomadic ghost ships drifting into shadows
to vanish then for good in paperless frontiers...

...as did the Rosary beads, though never far,
neglected safely in the bedroom drawer...

...but always apples-- not GMO bananas.
Tasty and apple-ish, crabby apples forever,
raised in the blood-shot sight of tipsy priests
who scolded boys for the riches of erections,
and blessed the swollen girls with bad advice.

Spritual fathers of ever worse behaviors--
Die Shadenfreude that ripened into pleasures—

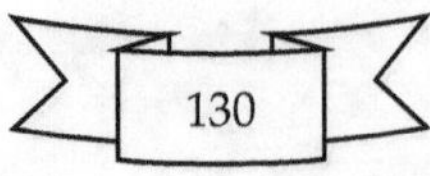

yet nothing like what creeps so near the tribe,
these DNA jolts of strange and Impossible Burgers.

Bananas, popping up impossibly in apples,
sticky fingers, pointing out from that darkness
where history oozes deep in sap, pointing hard
at the rings, round circles reaching centuries past
to a spot high up, or a ball, in the tree there,
a greedy aunt Clair, an odd Leif for a coward
outed now but rooted so long as a hero.

And should we go on, insisting, Guineos Manzanos?
My mother was our mother, an apple sure.

She raised us in a woods where wild apples,
my siblings, despair, and I, I firmly declare
these labels fashionable, revisionist history.

Today we are within what we wished for then,
down deep in our imagination the same as when
we acted in school on stages; costumes glittered,
sparkling new worlds and bright with treasures found.
We found a place in each, a spot of home,
and were never strange or lost inside ourselves.

Tod Perry

OCTOPUS MAN

On legs two or eight
they walk off of late
a mind each its own.

My unwise children
whimsies unchallenged
heads full and certain.

I want them back all
by the nose or the toes
by the ears so they listen

not replies like whatever
links to click added
on ways to live smarter.

Apps for E-wizards
mobile maps for survival
saving time, stretching wages.

Tools to watch closer
what I did as I'm doing
the things I made grosser.

Realtime suggestions

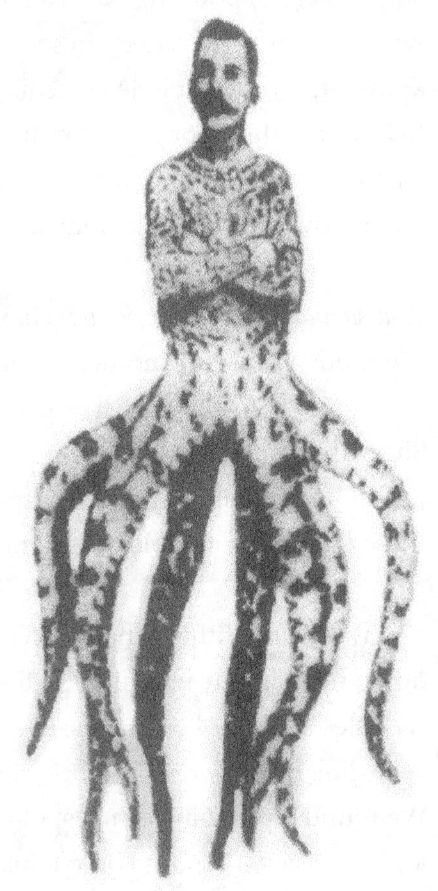

words bent to new meanings
with pop up corrections,

much smarter, they argue,
than words chosen once
from the soul long ago,

words that stood clear,
sturdy as spoken
that hang in the air
now grayer, said faded

in weight as in levity,
zero rated for gravity.

So the chimera ages,
a sideburn is thinner
grows bristles, he sags,

he's the octopus man
a white egg that floats
yet walks on his aches

slow as a wobble
nowhere to go
just hang out and dangle

while a pandemic infection
knocks old on its knees,

and young have less fun

a viral invasion
into lives never simple,
a climate in countdown

on legs still so little
how far can they run,
hey diddle diddle.

SOUTHERN SENIOR CARE

He sucks tubes for oxygen. Still alive.
Straddles gently the wasp in his prostate.
A widow lets the bitter thrive
nursing seeds that turn into hate.

Each breath is pain. It attacks from behind.
A vulture hops near to peck the liver.
Rooms of stale air sigh in hot days,
white heads hangover, soft music croons.

The masks on the walkers
one face for all tensions,
pass danger by inches,
a miracle so many
still shake on their feet,

or quiet, compliant,
on wheelchairs worn out
in shadows sweating
so long as pills last
tongues hung sideways
dogs in the heat.

Crumbs in the toaster
an age in disorder

stones fly off bridges,
dams set to buckle,
past care long ago

flush out of funds,
old music slow words
soft worms for the ear
replay and repeat
downstream disaster
it never grows old.

WOUND WHISPERER

Some wounds too deep don't want to heal. A heart
that hangs on shallow promises might never knit.
This wrist is a fractured nest, torn feathers clinging,
thin spikes in splintered bones, all writhing hopes
clamped to an arm betrayed, to a fist of fingers
so spindly and fragile it cannot crawl away.
Blue stones in mummy cloth and wrapped so tight
it's bound to radiate in pain for centuries.

It tingles in storms, when cold or shadows cross,
grows hot with stings for an unwilling skeleton,
bones sparking fire, then turning blue again,
a crab claw pegged on a crucifix of ice.

The morning's hope soon drains in fading spirals,
poor wine, it quickly scrapes the throat
with harsher tastes to burn, endlessly worse,
ever duller and never better any hour.

Until you appeared like calm to mend the pieces,
wound whisperer with kindness for a thirsty soul
the timely rains to soothe this waiting cactus,
with sure hands and the steadiest of hearts that heal,
to unfold, feather by feather, the wings of a phoenix.

SECTION SIX:
NEW POEMS, 2025

 INFLECTION WHIPLASH

Growing next door to the dunes
our legs wild as waves in the ocean;
our dreams rode on winds to the east
we clammed in all tides by the gulls.

Squawking the long ways past Montauk
south of Brooklyn beyond Nantucket
barrier islands stretched under Long Island
all sand to the tip then out the Atlantic.

The dunes long gone are sand under mansions,
dirt beneath weeds to be paved over soon,

So Berlin in its changes could dazzle the eyes:
goose steps to borscht, fur caps with red stars
just pennies on sale by the wall or the Ku'dam,
its bouquets of light warmed nights at their bluest
and a city that flared through the dark into dawn
then danced home late on high silver heels.

A new dawn now rises, it whispers and murmurs
ever closer like thunder in swarms on dark wings
with blood for our hands,
                not yet in our eyes,
still open to wonder with sparkle, with hope,

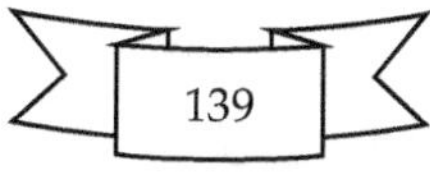

no matter the murders of crows in the sky,
the flotillas of drones not far from today,
dropping down slowly they glow in the dawn,
the fiery sparking waves of new empires
in dawns so black now dressed for orphans
drowning in the warp at the end of one era
or in webs of tall waves as another tide rises.

THE QUIET KISS OF TIME

Quiet as the wish for a kiss
moonlight flickers smoothly over water
no telling if its secrets come ashore
or drift forever out to sea.

In old hotels with long porches by the shore
the places travelers came to from afar
for peaceful evenings long ago their laughter
danced and rose up with the smoke into the air.

I heard them as a child at night
refugees from wars a world away
some distance near me but never far
their evenings hang like fruit
beyond their time still full.

The nights, the rooms remain
except they're out of season
such rooms are not the same when empty,
can never be the same at all,
their secrets out of reach, remembered
most beautiful once more to touch.
I may not be returning there again.